DOMESTIC ABUSE AND VIOLENCE IN THE COVID-19 PANDEMIC

The Dark Side of the Lockdown

DOMESTIC ABUSE AND VIOLENCE IN THE COVID-19 PANDEMIC

The Dark Side of the Lockdown

SAUN-JAYE S. BROWN
June 2021.

TAMARiND HiLL
.PRESS

County Durham

Copyright © Tamarind Hill Press 2022

County Durham, United Kingdom

The moral right of Saun-Jaye S. Brown to be identified as the author of this work has been asserted in accordance with the Copyright, Design and Patents Act of 1988.

All rights reserved. No part of this publication may be reproduced, stored in a retrievable system, or transmitted in any form or by any means, electronic, mechanical photocopying, recording or otherwise, without the permission of the author and copyright owner.

This book is not intended as a substitute or replacement for the advice of counsellors or other professionals. The publisher is not responsible for any goods and/or services offered or referred to in this book and expressly disclaim all liability in connection with the fulfilment of orders for any such goods and/or services and for any damage, loss, or expense to person or property arising out of or relating to them.

ISBN:
978-1-915161-27-7

TAMARiND HiLL
.PRESS

Table of Contents

Introduction 6

Chapter One 10

Cases of Domestic Violence During the COVID-19 Lockdown in both Developed and Developing Countries 10

Chapter Two 26

COVID-19 Pandemic and Same-sex Relationships 26

Chapter Three 38

Access to help for domestic violence during COVID-19 38

Conclusion 46

References 51

Introduction

Domestic abuse is a public health issue that affects people all over the world. It manifests itself in a variety of ways, with serious physical and psychological effects for the victim and their entire family. Domestic abuse is a cycle of forceful, controlling behaviour that affects people of all gender, ages, sexual orientations, races, ethnicities, religions, social classes, and immigration statuses in our community.

Domestic abuse encompasses a wide range of acts of violence: physical, sexual, and emotional (Hegarty et al., 2000). And while it is most commonly associated with violence between male and female partners, with heterosexual women being more likely to report it, it can also include violence between same sex partners and transgender people, which is likely to be underreported.

As the coronavirus pandemic wreaked havoc on people's lives and economies across the globe in March of 2020, governments all over the world started issuing stay-at-home or shelter-in-place orders to help stem the virus's spread. While these measures were put in place with the best of intentions, being restricted to one's home away from family and friends, schools, and the work environment—the former of which was severely hit by closed businesses and rising unemployment—tended to raise tension and anxiety.

While these measures seemed plausible from a public health standpoint, there was major concern that they could lead to other negative outcomes, such as child abuse and domestic violence. Why? Because parents and children were now confined to their homes with no access to those who could spot signs of abuse and violence and/or provide the help or support needed to break away from these violent conditions (Aizer, 2010; Anderberg et al., 2016; Bhalotra et al., 2020b). The combination of stay-at-home measures and the pandemic's economic impact intensified the factors that are correlated with domestic violence. Factors such as decreased financial security due to unemployment, stress from childcare and home-schooling, and maladaptive coping methods. All of these factors, as well as others, increase the risk of abuse or intensify the level of violence among partners, especially women who have previously experienced violence from male partners, as well as violence from previously non-violent partners.

With the imposed nationwide lockdowns to prevent the virus from spreading, it has had social, psychological, and economic effects. Domestic violence or intimate partner violence (IPV) being one of those effects that have risen exponentially as a result of the COVID-19 pandemic's hidden costs. The rise in domestic violence cases was one of them (United Nations, 2020). However, there are significant challenges in data when it comes to analysing global patterns of domestic violence (DV).

Firstly, there is insufficient comparative data that can be used to establish cross-country comparisons (Jayachandran, 2015). Secondly, because of the private nature of domestic violence cases, most occurrences stay hidden and unreported, without their being any police records or surveys (Aizer, 2010).

Lastly, even when data is available, there is a substantial delay between the occurrence of offenses and the accessibility of data for researchers, limiting any study of the COVID-19 pandemic's impact on domestic violence.

Chapter One

Cases of Domestic Violence During the COVID-19 Lockdown in both Developed and Developing Countries

While some couples were able to rediscover marital bliss in the aftermath of the coronavirus pandemic lockdown by devoting more time to an emotional bond and connection with families, thereby improving unity, domestic violence has become a severe public health risk. Journalistic records from around the world suggest that there is marital struggle and turmoil, as domestic violence and divorce rates more than tripled in the first two months of 2020.

Roughly 20 people are physically abused by their intimate partner every minute in the United States, according to the National Coalition Against Domestic Violence. Domestic violence is the leading cause of violent crime in the United

States, accounting for 15% of all violent crimes. Intimate partner abuse affects one out of every four women and one out of every nine men. But with the coronavirus pandemic, home isolation orders provide abusers with greater opportunities to hurt victims, who are made more vulnerable by their inaccessibility to support systems and fewer choices for escaping the house.

Domestic abuse cases are on the rise in several locations, particularly among underprivileged communities, according to data. Take the Middle East and North Africa, for example, which have the fewest laws protecting women from domestic violence in the world. The United Nations identified a surge in gender-based violence as a result of COVID-19 in the Palestinian territories and warned that the coronavirus pandemic will disproportionately harm women, worsen already gendered risks and vulnerabilities, and deepen disparities.

Before the COVID-19 lockdown, statistics on cases of domestic violence against women were high, but with the lockdown measures put in place by most national governments, things were made worse. The World Health Organization (WHO), for example, in 2017, estimated that 1-in-3 (35%) women globally, have faced physical and/or sexual intimate partner violence or non-partner sexual violence at some point in their lives. In addition, WHO further reported that majority of domestic violence cases are intimate partner violence with approximately 38% of women being murdered by their male partner.

An analysis of the occurrence of domestic violence cases in Arab countries observed a lifetime experience to any sort of intimate partner violence of 73.3%, 35.6% physical intimate partner violence, 22% sexual intimate partner violence, and 49.8% emotional/psychological intimate partner violence. In addition, according to a multilevel study conducted in Nigeria in 2019, over one in four women (23.6%) have experienced intimate partner violence, with one in five, that is 20%, having encountered any type of intimate partner violence.

Domestic abuse cases climbed by 25-33% worldwide in 2020, as reported by the American Journal of Emergency Medicine. Domestic abuse calls in Jefferson County, Missouri, spiked by 27% in March 2020 in comparison to March 2019. Other cities in the United States, such as Portland, San Antonio, and New York, followed suit.

According to media reports from several Chinese cities, there was an increase in separation and domestic violence in March of 2020. As per the Shanghai-based online journal Sixth Tone, police in one county near the epicentre of the pandemic, Wuhan, had 162 reports of domestic violence in February, which is more than triple the 47 incidents reported in the same month the previous year.

In keeping with the reports of domestic violence cases around the world, it was reported by Ana Bella, founder of an NGO, that within the first two weeks of the lockdown in Spain, the emergency line for IPV received 18% more calls than in the same time one month before. Nonetheless, the French police reported a 30% increase in domestic violence complaints across the country in just one day. Cases of domestic violence in the southwest region of the country increased by 20%, according to Avon and Somerset, despite the fact that the lockdown was implemented later on. The National Domestic Violence Hotline in the United States reported that an increasing number of callers have reported their abusers using COVID-19 to further isolate their victims from friends and family, threatening to throw them out on the street if they get sick, and withholding financial resources or medical assistance.

Similarly, in Lebanon, according to Lewis, 60% of the women who phoned the KAFA hotline, a Lebanese women's safety non-governmental organization, in March, reported new incidences of physical assault or psychological abuse committed during the lockdown. Director of the Abaad Resource centre for gender equality in Lebanon, Ghida Anani, stated that the centre was receiving more calls regarding women fearing for their lives because of domestic violence which is on the rise in the home. As after presenting with flu-like symptoms which are associated with COVID-19, an average of approximately two women have been threatened by their family members.

Correspondingly, Feng Yuan, a co-founder of a non-profit in Beijing, put forward that underlying violent impulses that were there previously but weren't being displayed are highlighted because of the lockdown. Taub, supporting other theories, also suggested that the increase in domestic violence cases during the COVID-19 lockdown could be due to the broken support network, making it more difficult for victims to seek assistance. Various news reports have attributed the cause to a variety of factors, including marital frustrations, financial issues, screen time, homework, childcare, cheating, a lack of personal space, and stress from quarantine.

Though several developed countries have reported cases of domestic violence since the COVID-19 lockdown, African countries have yet to provide much official insight. Only a few countries in Africa have reported cases of domestic violence and these are minimal. Consequently, if this issue is not handled alongside the coronavirus pandemic, African countries may face additional public health and mental health issues in the future. As a result, addressing COVID-19 as a domestic violence contributing factor in tandem with the global community's attempts to stymie the pandemic's spread through biomedical and epidemiological methodologies not only adopts a systematic approach to ending the pandemic's adverse effects, but also aids in the facilitation of the pandemic's end.

Even though several African countries implemented a lockdown and stay-at-home order and the requirement of wearing face masks, washing hands for approximately one minute, and social distancing to prevent the virus from spreading, there have been reports of domestic violence against women. Google searches on domestic violence cases in Africa has risen since the beginning of the coronavirus pandemic. There has been an increase in the number of persons needing help in handling domestic violence according to these searches.

A report on Egypt conducted by the UNDP Gender and Justice reveals that there is no Egyptian law that openly references domestic violence. Accordingly, though some domestic violence offenses may be criminal under the Penal Code and Law No. 6 of 1998, they are only punishable if they go outside the appropriate restrictions of punishment as proposed by the judge. Also, whether the sustained injuries are noticeable when the complaint is filed at the police station. In contrast, Article 60, which is recognized as the husband's right to punish his wife as he sees fit, can still be used by the perpetrator to be acquitted provided he acted in good intentions.

With court trials throughout the country being postponed, it has resulted in a rise in the number of partners who have committed heinous acts of domestic violence against their partners. As a result of the COVID-19 lockdown, according to a report by the Egyptian Centre for Women's

Rights (ECWR), there has been an increase in conflict in the family conflict and instances of violence, accounting for 43% of the total number of 1146 cases received, with women accounting for over 70% of the complaints. According to another study, family issues have risen by 33%, family violence by 19%, and 11% of wives having been subjected to abuse from their husbands. Women have frequently cited being dependent on their husband as a determinant in domestic violence during the lockdown period, revealing the unequal structure of the relationship that typifies abuses in the home.

Domestic violence is still condoned by many Egyptians, as it is in many other African and Middle Eastern countries. As a result, Egypt's ranking as the world's second-worst country for sexual harassment, behind Afghanistan, is not coincidental. According to a research conducted by the Ministry of Health, about half of all women surveyed in Egypt had suffered some type of DV. Domestic violence survivors who were interviewed by Amnesty International characterized their partners' horrific physical and psychological abusive behaviour as the most common form of violence they had witnessed, claiming that their partners had assaulted, lashed, and burned them, as well as forcefully locking them inside the house. In a similar line, according to a survey conducted by Egypt's National Council of Women (ENCW), around 1.5 million women are subjected to domestic violence each year.

In comparison to other continents with a larger number of recorded cases and fatalities from the pandemic, Africa has been comparatively fortunate in terms of the coronavirus outbreak. However, it is more concerning because the continent that is experiencing the dormant effects of the COVID-19 lockdown cannot be easily evaluated. Most African countries, for example, declared a state of emergency in March 2020. Though some African countries began their shutdown with a few large cities, others issued a continent-wide lockdown.

Prior to the COVID-19 outbreak, the number of domestic violence cases, specifically that of gender-based violence reported in South Africa was one of the world's highest. According to statistics, on average, a woman is killed every three hours in South Africa, with numerous women, before they are killed, suffering assault and rape. Riots had already erupted in most sections of the country as a result of this phenomenon. In September of 2019, this gained attention from the South African government, which recognized the deplorable state that the nations' women were in and declared gender-based violence and femicide a national disaster.

According to sources, around 148 persons were detained and convicted of offences linked to gender-based violence during the coronavirus lockdown, more than 2,000 reports of gender-based violence were submitted to the South African Police Service in the first seven days of the country's lockdown. In addition, the gender-based violence National Command Centre, which oversees a national call centre, reported receiving approximately 12,000 calls regarding domestic violence since the lockdown was implemented. Additionally, there were claims of women being raped in temporary homeless shelters that were set up as part of the COVID-19 control measures.

Nonetheless, the government of South Africa is among the very few in Africa to implement extremely tight rules to prevent domestic violence during the lockdown. Such measures were put in place because the government banned the selling of cigarettes and alcohol, both of which have been linked to the spread of domestic violence.

Most countries have implemented public health initiatives to reduce the danger of COVID-19 transmission and spreading. Many of these measures are being implemented throughout the Caribbean, including "stay at home" orders and the shutdown of entertainment and relaxing areas like clubs and beaches. Although these steps are necessary to prevent the spreading of COVID-19, they may elevate the number of occurrences of domestic violence.

According to a 2018 UNDOC report on Gender-related Killing of Women and Girls, women have a higher probability of being killed in the home. One in every three women homicide victims is killed by an intimate partner, and approximately one in every four is killed by other family members. Per the report, 85% of women who are killed in Guyana was by an intimate partner or was a family-related homicide. Correspondingly, 90% of victims of intimate partner violence in Jamaica were women; and approximately one-third of female homicide in Trinidad and Tobago was intimate partner violence and family-related.

There's no denying that the spread of diseases and infirmities affects people in diverse ways. As a result, it is projected that the COVID-19 outbreaks will affect all susceptible groups in different ways. With that said, although an increase in domestic violence is observed in every country, the lockdown to stymie the spread of the virus, there are more reports of cases in developed countries reported than in developing countries.

There is diverse evidence arising from researches carried out regarding the effect of the COVID-19 pandemic on domestic violence globally, as well as information from police reports and helplines. However, the impact of the outbreak on domestic violence remains ambiguous, as there is not enough significant data that provides insight into all cases across countries. Likewise, in some countries and cultures, certain acts are not seen as domestic violence, but rather the right to discipline. One thing is clear, however, and it is that domestic violence is on the rise given the lockdown measures implemented to stem the spread of the virus.

Chapter Two
COVID-19 Pandemic and Same-sex Relationships

According to The National Intimate Partner and Sexual Violence Survey conducted by the Centers for Disease Control and Prevention in 2010, it was indicated that LGBTQ participants report experiencing the same level or greater domestic violence than heterosexuals. Bisexual women, especially, were revealed to be more vulnerable to domestic violence. It was revealed that 61% of bisexual women report having been physically abused and/or stalked by their partner.

Abusers in heterosexual relationships utilize the same kind of controlling methods as LGBTQ abusers, however, based on their gender identity and sexual orientation, they experience unique methods of manipulation. Reporting abuse to social services can be made significantly harder for the abused, as the abuser, for one, may threaten to "out" their victim to their family.

Throughout every community, severe financial stress and increased unemployment can lead to domestic violence, but LGBTQ+ persons may be among those who are most at risk of an increase in domestic violence during the current pandemic. According to a new study from the LGBTQ advocacy group Human Rights Campaign, LGBTQ persons are more likely to work in sectors that are seriously impacted by the pandemic, than their heterosexual counterparts, and thus are more susceptible to financial insecurity. LGBTQ people are more likely to have a lower income, rely on government assistance, and lack access to health care (Whittington et al., 2020). Furthermore, LGBTQ people are more likely to have poor health and behavioural issues (Gonzales & Henning-Smith, 2017). Pre-existing diseases such as diabetes, cardiovascular disease, asthma, or HIV affect about 65% of LGBTQ individuals (Huelskoetter & Gee, 2017). Approximately 37% of LGBTQ adults smoke on a daily basis, as opposed to 27% of non-LGBTQ adults (Whittington et al., 2020). As a result of these circumstances, LGBTQ people are at a higher risk of serious illnesses from COVID-19 (CDC, 2020a). These different hazards and pressures can also affect the functioning of a couple's relationship (Pietromonaco & Overall, 2020).

Given this, it can lead to domestic abuse in the LGBTQ population. Similar to heterosexual relationships, being restricted at home, a partner who is prone to being physically, emotionally, or verbally abusive is more likely to be frustrated and irritated, putting the victim at a higher risk of repeated, or maybe more intense violence.

Although the exact effect of the coronavirus pandemic on same-sex relationships is unknown, gay, lesbian, bisexual, transgender, and queer (LGBTQ) people are facing increased minority stress as a result of persisting systemic injustice and new challenges posed by the pandemic. The persistent stigma and discrimination against the LGBTQ community has been amplified by conspiracy theories such as "God sent coronavirus to destroy LGBTQ people" (Li et al., 2020). There's also a lack of targeted public aid for this demographic (Gruberg, 2020).

According to Boyle et al. (2017) and Saltzman et al. (2020) social support and community relations are critical coping mechanisms during large-scale community crises. Many LGBTQ people, on the other hand, have lost their social support systems as a result of lockdowns and stay-at-home orders. Closures of schools limit LGBTQ students' access to campus resources and peer support (Burns, 2020; Salerno et al., 2020). Without the support of their families, older

LGBTQ people face social isolation and loneliness (Salerno et al., 2020; Seegert, 2020).

With the cancellation of numerous social and pride activities, opportunities to socialize with those who were supportive were restricted. Consequently, according to Blair and Holmberg (2008, 2019) with the decrease in outside interactions and social support, same-sex couples' relationship experiences were impacted, and it puts added pressure on romantic partners to cope with many stressors in such trying circumstances.

Baxter and Erbert (1999) put forward that crises are also defining moments in relationships, which are marked by critical decision and increased interpersonal conflict. The coronavirus pandemic has hastened couples' decision to move in together, to separate, or even to end the relationship because of social and economic difficulties (Fetters, 2020; Singer, 2020). With couples having varying points of view on these topics, it might lead to serious relationship challenges. Günther-Bel et al. (2020) argue that with the continued face-to-face interactions, individuals' limits are tested, and existing relational challenges are made more salient for couples quarantining together. Not being able to see their partner in person might cause relationship problems for individuals who are physically separated. As a result, dealing with those relationship issues is critical for the functioning of couples' relationship and individuals' coping with the pandemic.

To highlight the probable implications of the COVID-19 pandemic on romantic relationships, Pietromonaco and Overall (2020) offered a conceptual model. The vulnerability-stress-adaptation model (Karney & Bradbury, 1995) states that stress factors from the COVID-19 pandemic, pre-existing contextual vulnerabilities (e.g., social class, minority status), and enduring individual vulnerabilities (e.g., attachment insecurity, history of trauma) are likely to increase harmful dyadic relationship processes (e.g., withdrawal, hostility), which in turn undermine couples' relationship quality and stability. Individual and contextual sensitivity factors are also likely to enhance the pandemic's negative impacts on couples' communication and relationships (Pietromonaco & Overall, 2020).

With studies on trauma or life-threatening experiences, we are provided with insight into how the pandemic may impact same-sex relationships. According to Cohan and Cole (2020), the year after Hurricane Hugo, the divorce rate among heterosexual couples soared in the hardest-hit areas. Pietromonaco and Overall (2020) argues that this could be due to the enormous costs of rebuilding communities with regards to both time and money, which has resulted in chronic stress and growing relational disagreements, all of which add to the end of a relationship.

As maintained by Cohan et al. (2009), divorce rates, on the other hand, fell dramatically after the 9/11 attacks and the 1995 bombing of Oklahoma City (Nakonezny et al., 2004). These acts of terrorism had a greater death rate than Hurricane Hugo, which increased people's fear of the future and worry over their lives. When people's lives are threatened, they rely on their closest friends and family for consolation and protection, which could reflect why couples turned to one another and remained together following these terrorist attacks (Pietromonaco & Overall, 2020).

The course of the COVID-19 pandemic is unclear, as is the case with several natural disasters, necessitating the use of public health measures to achieve a more gradual increase and decrease in the number of cases and working toward modifying and regulating behaviour in order to encourage recovery. As a result, the ongoing pandemic might pose a threat to normal relational functioning. The overwhelming amount of unchecked COVID-19 pandemic-related fatalities, similar to terrorist attacks, has created a mindset of fear and uncertainty (Pietromonaco & Overall, 2020), implying a greater demand for personal relationships. Others, on the other hand, might well be hesitant to establish close relationships owing to pandemic fears. As a result, it's unknown if the COVID-19 epidemic will worsen or improve relationship health and stability.

The COVID-19 pandemic has led to decreased support networks for same-sex couples, as well as increased minority stress, financial challenges, and health inequalities, all of which can carry over into their relationships, resulting in relationship dissatisfaction and dissolution. According to Rostosky and Riggle (2017), same-sex couples have developed constructive practices in their relationships such as the sharing of house chores, positive attitudes and exchanges, and efficient communication and negotiation that protect them from daily stressors and problems. These beneficial characteristics may be kept amidst the current crisis and aid in mitigating the pandemic's negative consequences.

Li and Samp (2020) and Lannutti (2014) argue that avoiding arguments about relationship disclosure or same-sex marriage in same-sex relationships is correlated with poor mental wellbeing and relationship dissatisfaction. As a result, complaint avoidance is widely regarded as damaging in romantic relationships, destroying people's relationships and personal wellbeing.

Managing outside stressors, for example, increased minority stress, financial challenges, and health inequalities, and decreased physical activity, may take a toll on individual's energy and their communicative skills, which in turn makes it more difficult for partners to resolve relational issues in a constructive manner during the present crisis (Pietromonaco & Overall, 2020). Furthermore, Li and Samp (2019) and Worley and Samp (2016) postulate that given that the pandemic affects people's lives and their livelihoods, persons may fixate on matters that they deem "more important" while trivializing the seriousness of relationship issues, leading to increased complaint avoidance.

According to Satici et al. (2020), the COVID-19 pandemic has also raised concerns about interpersonal relationships and personal health. Increased perceived threat of difficult talks and increased subject avoidance have been connected to increased relational and illness uncertainties (Leustek & Theiss, 2018). Similarly, the heightened COVID-19-related ambiguity can drive people to avoid making complaints because they are afraid of the unfavourable effects of conflicts. As a result, increased negative effects of the pandemic and a greater perception of COVID-19 as a concern can indicate a higher rate of complaint avoidance, which can lead to negative relationship and personal results.

The exact effects of such individual and contextual agents on same-sex couples remain unclear in the current pandemic. Still, research has revealed that being separated or confined together may deplete couples' resources and limit opportunities for constructive conflict resolution, possibly lowering relationship quality (Pietromonaco & Overall, 2020). Combined with the difficulties brought on by the COVID-19 pandemic, these variables undermine the quality of same-sex couples' relationships and personal well-being.

Chapter Three
Access to help for domestic violence during COVID-19

As discussed previously, to stymie the spread of the COVID-19 pandemic, stay-at-home orders were issued in March of 2020. Schools were closed down and persons were laid off, or furloughed, while others started working from home. With the lockdown initiated, domestic violence, specifically intimate partner violence went on the rise. With people's mobility being restricted and having to be confined to their homes, numerous victims of domestic abuse were trapped with their abusers. As these regulations were enforced globally, the demand for services from domestic violence hotlines were expected to increase. However, for several organizations, it was the opposite. Experts on the subject found that the cases of domestic violence had not fallen, and the demand for help was not on the decrease but that victims could not safely contact these helplines. And while most travel bans have been relaxed, the pandemic and its impacts continue, and there is universal consensus that locations where caseloads have dropped are likely to face a second spike. During a crisis, inequalities in socioeconomic health factors are amplified, and sheltering in place may not cause equal suffering to everyone.

Domestic violence cannot be handled without addressing societal concerns, particularly in the setting of a pandemic that is isolating people.

Likewise, economic independence is an important aspect in preventing violence. Many people who are victims of domestic violence find that their financial entanglements with abusive partners are too complicated to break free from without a backup source of income. This will be seen with the higher rates of job loss and unemployment, especially in women of colour, immigrants, and those without a college education. With the restrictions imposed to tackle the virus' spread as mentioned before, people's access to safe havens have been hampered: shelters and hotels have reduced or closed their capacity, and travel restrictions have limited people's access to safe havens. Shelters have made tremendous efforts to relieve congestion and assist inhabitants in relocating to hotels, extended-stay flats, or relatives' and friends' homes.

Reporting cases of domestic violence may be made difficult during the pandemic. The filing of police reports can differ with each precinct. Some precincts may accept online reports while others involve in-person visitation. In the same way, individual trial courts also have the authority to decide how restraining orders are filed. Persons who seek assistance via the legal system may be discouraged by the lack of a clear and regular process for reporting abuse. When domestic violence intensifies, people of colour, who have long been subjected to police oppression and brutality, may be less likely than White people to seek assistance from the police.

The majority of persons who are affected by domestic violence do not seek assistance. When these persons visit hospitals and clinics, medical personnel have the opportunity to recognize these individuals, provide counselling, and even get them in touch with social services. Medical offices can be a secure location for victims of abuse to come forward. The result of physical exams, how the patient behaves while talking over physically intimate aspects of certain examinations (breast, pelvic, or rectal), or a partner who is hostile can all be indicators of possible intimate partner violence. When patients are alone in settings such as emergency rooms and labour and delivery rooms, policies require domestic violence screening. The inclusion of social workers, safety planning, and a review of services available to victims and their dependents are all possible during an evaluation in healthcare settings. However, this opportunity has often been non-existent in the COVID-19 era. Safely screening patients for domestic violence grew increasingly challenging as offices cancelled and delayed non-urgent visits and switched to telemedicine platforms. Persons affected by domestic violence and need medical assistance may not only reside in places where Internet or cellular coverage is unstable, but their attackers may listen in on their conversations, making it impossible for patients to report growing violence at home.

As a third wave of the COVID-19 pandemic threatens the world, several measures can be taken to improve and stimulate reasonable access to services for assistance. Firstly, communities can make sure that everyone has access to high-speed Internet in their homes. Wireless access points in public locations or a subsidy program similar to the Federal Communications Commission's Lifeline program could be used to improve access. Such approaches would not only increase telehealth access, but they would also allow people who have been affected by IPV to search for resources and maintain important social connections.

Secondly, continued screening for domestic violence and the discussion of safety planning can be done during telemedicine sessions. Providers can use structured questions to standardize screening and provide all patients with information, irrespective of whether they report domestic violence or not. Clinicians should also familiarize themselves with the services available in their communities. If the patient discloses abuse, then the clinician and the patient throughout the telemedicine consultation can establish signs to indicate that an abusive partner is present. For example, throwing things around while on a video call or pre-recorded comments on an audio call. Clinicians can go over safety procedures that patients can partake in when it is safe to hold discussions about domestic violence, for example, deleting Internet browsing history or messages and emails, saving helpline information under other listings, such as a grocery store or pharmacy listing, and setting up a new, confidential email account for receiving resource information or communicating with clinicians.

Lastly, when defining crisis standards of care, governing entities should address societal factors of health. The effect of domestic violence on persons is influenced by status, finances, and the availability of resources. The coronavirus pandemic has brought attention to a number of current public health concerns, including domestic abuse. Clinicians, public health authorities, and legislators must examine the layers of socioeconomic disparities in our communities and how they impact people's access to help and care as the COVID-19 measures and regulations ease as we begin to live this new kind of normal. Lastly, when defining crisis standards of care, governing entities should address societal factors of health. When another public health crisis strikes, the pandemic has underlined the level of effort that needs to be put into ensuring that persons who have been abused continue to have access to assistance, refuge, and medical care.

Conclusion

It is important to note that well before the outbreak of the coronavirus, domestic violence was a worldwide pandemic. As per the data gathered by the United Nations, on a global scale, 243 million women and girls, ages 15 to 49 suffered physical or sexual abuse at the hands of an intimate partner in the previous twelve months. In other words, one out of every three women has been a victim of physical or sexual abuse at some point in their lives. Persons who identify as LGBTQ+ face equal levels of violence.

Many families over the world have been compelled to cohabitate, indicating a true "emergency within an emergency." The statistical data that has surfaced from China, now that the severe isolation measures have come to a stop (for the time being), has produced an increase in reports of domestic violence, particularly among women who have been forced to live in abusive relationships for months. Many publications reported on instances of spousal violence, which was followed by intense child maltreatment. Forced seclusion in cramped rooms or households, such as those in China, where there was a constant fear of maltreatment, resulted in a tremendous deal of stress and psychological trauma. Furthermore, because of the requirement to address public order issues, there was a paucity of police surveillance for this form of abuse. As the emergency grew, there was a rush to buy firearms and alcohol in the United States (a dangerous combination).

What effect will all of this have on a family who is now trapped at home with an abuser? In certain countries, for example, Italy, where the emergency and isolation measures are still in effect, we are seeing the polar opposite, with a decrease in calls to toll-free anti-violence helplines. It is evident that the drop in complaints does not indicate a decrease in violent episodes, but rather that the greatest risk during the COVID-19 pandemic is that the victim is locked within the home with the abuser, with no way out and no way to contact outside aid. The same is true for children who have been the victims of violence and have been isolated from attending school due to abuse reported by instructors or friends.

Domestic violence or intimate partner violence is a worldwide public health issue with significant social and economic effects. In times of crisis, severe unemployment, and social stress, cases of domestic violence can further increase. There is, however, a lack of essential information in countries, to quickly develop public policies to control the crisis. Timely data from police reports and domestic violence service calls suffers from significant under-reporting.

Alternatively, observational data on domestic violence cases, is rarely quickly accessible and is expensive. This research recommends tracking the incidence of domestic violence using publicly available data from Google searches, for example. This data has several advantages. It is free of cost, fast, accessible on a daily basis, and it enables for cross-regional comparisons.

People's dependence on technology has risen, and the manner in which mental health, legal, and other social services are offered to persons who have experienced or are experiencing domestic violence and are unwilling to leave their homes has changed as a result of social distancing. As the criminal justice system has been disrupted, governments have changed to virtual court proceedings, facilitated online means for getting protection orders, and declared their plans to continue providing legal protection to victims.

Countries must encourage the development of alternative reporting systems, expand the availability of shelter choices, enhance the security and justice systems' power, retain important reproductive healthcare services, where victims of domestic violence are frequently recognized and supported, and finance economic security measures for same-sex relationship persons, especially if serving on the front lines of the pandemic.

COVID-19 is an external shock that is having a considerable impact on the global incidence of domestic violence. While no one could have foreseen such a spike in the number of instances around the world, it is now time for law enforcement agencies, governments, and society as a whole to work together to develop effective methods to prevent COVID-19's negative impacts on domestic violence.

References

Aizer, A. (2010). The gender wage gap and domestic violence. *American Economic Review, 100 (4)*, 1847–59.

Anderberg, D., Rainer, H., Wadsworth, J., & Wilson, T. (2016) Unemployment and domestic violence: Theory and evidence. *The Economic Journal, 126(597)*, 1947–1979.

Baxter, L. A., & Erbert, L. A. (1999). Perceptions of dialectical contradictions in turning points of development in heterosexual romantic relationships. *Journal of Social and Personal Relationships, 16(5)*, 547–569. https://doi.org/10.1177/0265407599165001

Bhalotra, S., Britto, D., Pinotti, P., & Sampaio, B. (2020) Job displacement, unemployment benefits and domestic violence.

Blair, K. L., & Holmberg, D. (2008). Perceived social network support and well-being in same-sex versus mixed-sex romantic relationships. *Journal of Social and Personal Relationships, 25(5)*, 769–791. https://doi.org/10.1177/0265407508096695

Blair, K. L., & Holmberg, D. (2019). What would you know about it? Managing ingroup vs. outgroup perceived support of same-sex vs. mixed-sex romantic relationships. *Journal of GLBT Family Studies, 15(5)*, 429–441. https://doi.org/10.1080/1550428X.2018.1563760

Boyle, S. C., LaBrie, J. W., Costine, L. D., & Witkovic, Y. D. (2017). "It's how we deal": Perceptions of LGB peers' use of alcohol and other drugs to cope and sexual minority adults' own coping motivated substance use following the Pulse nightclub shooting. *Addictive Behaviors, 65*, 51–55. https://doi.org/10.1016/j.addbeh.2016.10.001

CDC. (2020a, September 11). Coronavirus disease 2019 (COVID-19): People with certain medical conditions. https://www.cdc.gov/coronavirus/2019-ncov/need-extra-precautions/people-with-medical-conditions.html

Cohan, C. L., & Cole, S. W. (2002). Life course transitions and natural disaster: Marriage, birth, and divorce following Hurricane Hugo. *Journal of Family Psychology, 16(1)*, 14–25. https://doi.org/10.1037//0893-3200.16.1.14

Cohan, C. L., Cole, S. W., & Schoen, R. (2009). Divorce following the September 11 terrorist attacks. *Journal of Social and Personal Relationships, 26(4)*, 512–530. https://doi.org/10.1177/0265407509351043

Fetters, A. (2020, July 17). Move in? Get divorced? The pandemic forces couples to decide: Romantic partners are emerging from quarantine with a newfound sense of clarity. *The New York Times.* https://www.nytimes.com/2020/07/17/opinion/coronavirus-relationships-decisions.html

Gonzales, G., & Henning-Smith, C. (2017). Health disparities by sexual orientation: Results and implications from the behavioral risk factor surveillance system. *Journal of Community Health, 42(6)*, 1163–1172. https://doi.org/10.1007/s10900-017-0366-z

Gruberg, S. (2020, April 9). An effective response to the coronavirus requires targeted assistance for LGBTQ people. Center for American Progress. https://www.americanprogress.org/issues/lgbtq-rights/news/2020/04/09/482895/effective-response-coronavirus-requires-targeted-assistance-lgbtq-people/

Günther-Bel, C., Vilaregut, A., Carratala, E., Torras-Garat, S., & Pérez-Testor, C.

(2020). A mixed-method study of individual, couple, and parental functioning during the state-regulated COVID-19 lockdown in Spain. *Family Process, 59(3)*, 1060–1079. https://doi.org/10.1111/famp.12585

Huelskoetter, T., & Gee, E. (2017, June 9). Senate repeal bill would still eviscerate coverage and protections for people with pre-existing conditions. Center for American Progress. https://www.americanprogress.org/issues/healthcare/news/2017/06/09/433871/senate-repeal-bill-still-eviscerate-coverage-protections-people-pre-existing-conditions/

Jayachandran, S. (2015). The roots of gender inequality in developing countries. Economics, 7 (1):63–88.

Karney, B. R., & Bradbury, T. N. (1995). The longitudinal course of marital quality and stability: A review of theory, method, and research. *Psychological Bulletin, 118(1)*, 3–

34. https://doi.org/10.1037/0033-2909.118.1.3

Lannutti, P. J. (2014). *Experiencing same-sex marriage: Individuals, couples, and social networks.* Peter Lang Publishing.

Leustek, J., & Theiss, J. A. (2018). Features of illness versus features of romantic relationships as predictors of cognitive and behavioral coping among individuals with type 2 diabetes. *Health Communication, 33(12)*, 1549–1559. https://doi.org/10.1080/10410236.2017.1384346

Li, Y., & Samp, J. A. (2020). Antecedents to and outcomes of same-sex couples' coming out talk. *Western Journal of Communication, 85(1)*, 1–21. https://doi.org/10.1080/10570314.2020.1748702

Nakonezny, P. A., Reddick, R., & Rodgers, J. L. (2004). Did divorces decline after the Oklahoma City bombing? *Journal of*

Marriage and Family, 66(1), 90–100. http://www.jstor.org/stable/3599868

Pietromonaco, P. R., & Overall, N. C. (2020). Applying relationship science to evaluate how the COVID-19 pandemic may impact couples' relationships. *American Psychologist.* Advance online publication. https://doi.org/10.1037/amp0000714

Rostosky, S. S., & Riggle, E. D. B. (2017). Same-sex couple relationship strengths: A review and synthesis of the empirical literature (2000–2016). *Psychology of Sexual Orientation and Gender Diversity, 4(1)*, 1–13. https://doi.org/10.1037/sgd0000216

Salerno, J. P., Williams, N. D., & Gattamorta, K. A. (2020). LGBTQ populations: Psychologically vulnerable communities in the COVID-19 pandemic. *Psychological Trauma: Theory, Research, Practice, and Policy, 12(S1)*, S239–S242. https://doi.org/10.1037/tra0000837

Saltzman, L. Y., Hansel, T. C., & Bordnick, P. S. (2020). Loneliness, isolation, and social support factors in post-COVID-19 mental health. *Psychological Trauma: Theory, Research, Practice, and Policy, 12(S1)*, S55–S57. https://doi.org/10.1037/tra0000703

Satici, B., Saricali, M., Satici, S. A., & Griffiths, M. D. (2020). Intolerance of uncertainty and mental wellbeing: Serial mediation by rumination and fear of COVID-19. *International Journal of Mental Health and Addiction.* Advance online publication. https://doi.org/10.1007/s11469-020-00305-0

Seegert, L. (2020, April 22). COVID-19 is hitting older LGBTQ adults especially hard. Association of Health Care Journalists. https://healthjournalism.org/blog/2020/04/COVID-19-is-hitting-older-lgbtq-adults-especially-hard/

Singer, J. (2020, May 20). Are couples who moved in together for quarantine okay? Glamour. https://www.glamour.com

/story/are-couples-who-moved-in-together-for-quarantine-okay

Whittington, C., Hadfield, K., & Calderón, C. (2020). The lives and livelihoods of many in the LGBTQ community are at risk amidst COVID-19 crisis. Human Rights Campaign Foundation. https://www.hrc.org/resources/the-lives-and-livelihoods-of-many-in-the-lgbtq-community-are-at-risk-amidst-COVID-19-crisis

Worley, T. R., & Samp, J. (2016). Complaint avoidance and complaint-related appraisals in close relationships: A dyadic power theory perspective. *Communication Research, 43(3)*, 391–413. https://doi.org/10.1177/0093650214538447

www.ingramcontent.com/pod-product-compliance
Lightning Source LLC
Chambersburg PA
CBHW071544080526
44588CB00011B/1793